The Five Pillars

How to Find Your People, Place & Purpose

**By
David Lamb**

Acknowledgements

Thank you to Sonya, Jessica, Isabella and Will. I love you and am grateful for your love, encouragement, and example to live life to the fullest.

To my big family, thank you for the way you love, lead and live.

Thank you, mom, Archie, Larry, Elisha, Tina, Debbie, Karen, Sandy, and Tammy. My life has been blessed with amazing colleagues, co-workers, bosses, and friends.

Thank you to everyone who pushed me to do better, reach higher and give more.

Dedication

This book is dedicated to my brother, Michael Vernon Lamb. I miss you and think of you every day.

Special Thanks...

A special thank you to my editor Sheri Rose. Your patience, encouragement and talent made this happen. I will be forever grateful!

The Five Pillars

How to Find Your People, Place and Purpose

By
David Lamb

First Edition
First Printing, 2022

Book Cover Credits:
Final design & production by Anna Harmon,
Edited by Sheri Rose, and Candice Lawrence, Athens,
Georgia

ISBN: 9798986843483
Shades Creek Press, LLC

Printed in the United States of America
All rights reserved. No part of this book may be used or reproduced in any manner, including internet usage, without express written consent of the author or publisher.

Disclaimer

Unless otherwise indicated, all the names, characters, businesses, places, events, and incidents in this book are either the product of the author's imagination, used in a fictitious manner, or used by permission granted by the individuals. Any resemblance to actual persons, living or dead, or actual events is purely coincidental.

Table of Contents

INTRODUCTION 3
PILLAR 1: COMPELLING VISION 7
   SUE MARTIN 7
   YOUR COMPELLING VISION 11
On the Right Path.. 12
Off the Wrong Path... 13
Port in a Storm 14
   PILLAR TALK 1 14
Compelling Vision: Questions and Action Steps . 15
PILLAR 2: HEALTHY LIFESTYLE............................... 18
   MICHELLE STEINKE-BAUMGARD 19
   YOUR HEALTHY LIFESTYLE 22
The Body Is a Wonderland 23
What's Good for the Body Is Good for the Mind 23
Look Good, Feel Good, Live Good....................... 24
   PILLAR TALK 2 25
Healthy Lifestyle: Questions and Action Steps ... 26
PILLAR 3: RICH RELATIONSHIPS 29
   BILLY BAKER... 29
   CREATING RICH RELATIONSHIPS 31
Toxic Cleanse 33
Life-Giving Relationships...................................... 34
Intentionality 35
Do All You Can Do, Then Let It Go....................... 36
   PILLAR TALK 3 39
Rich Relationships: Questions and Action Steps. 40

- PILLAR 4: FULFILLING CAREER 43
  - CAROL GARDNER 43
  - FINDING YOUR FULFILLING CAREER 46
- Lead With Passion 46
- Second Nature 47
- Market Demand 48
  - PILLAR TALK 4 51
- Fulfilling Career: Questions and Action Steps 51
- PILLAR 5: BIG MISSION 57
  - RODNEY SMITH 57
  - YOUR BIG MISSION 59
- Focus on Others 60
- Attitude of Gratitude 60
- Legacy 61
  - PILLAR TALK 5 62
- Big Mission: Questions and Action Steps 65
- EPILOGUE 71
  - BOLL WEEVILS 71
  - WHAT'S YOUR BOLL WEEVIL? 72

Lamb/5 Pillars

INTRODUCTION

On October 18, 2018, just after five in the afternoon, doctors instructed my family to say our goodbyes to my older brother Mike. He passed away just a few hours later at the age of 61, and I'm still not good with it. This book is my attempt to make something good out of a painful loss.

Mike's official cause of death was from heart issues and diabetes complications. However, I am certain that Mike's heart gave up long before it ever gave out. As painful as Mike's passing was, it neither shocked nor surprised me. He died a slow death, emotionally and physically wasting away. As I sit here, I still regret being unable to wake Mike from his slumber and help him fight his way back to health and wholeness.

I see people every day who struggle like Mike. Maybe because of Mike's passing, I'm more aware of them. There have even been several times when I have struggled to find my place and purpose. I believe we all have been there at one time or another. Maybe you are there right now.

The reality is that life can be hard. Every day good people are dealt tough blows, sometimes in multiples, and they are tempted to give up. Sadly, every day many do give up. Honest, hardworking people throw in the towel, accept their fate, and resign themselves to just make it through another day.

Despite the harshness of reality, I'm convinced that hope is the better way. It may be buried beneath hardship, heartache, loss, and struggle, but you and I both know there's a better way. If you didn't, you never would have picked up this book. Life is worth living. *Your* life is worth living. I will never discount your past or current experience, but I'm here to tell you that if you have breath, you have a purpose. As I sit here, I'm confident that all our lives are not only worth living, but they can be our best work yet.

For most of my adult life, I have worked as a broadcast journalist. In that role, I have had the honor of meeting and interviewing many of the most influential and successful politicians, business leaders, and sports giants. My career experience has shown that the most successful people have a pattern to their lives that includes living out The Five Pillars outlined in this book:

1. Compelling Vision
2. Healthy Lifestyle
3. Rich Relationships
4. Fulfilling Career
5. Big Mission

Those who crush life win at most, if not all, of The Five Pillars. Those who get crushed miss the mark for most, if not all, of them. Just as success has a formula, failure does too. I'm dead set on finding the formula for a life that is full of passion, purpose, and impact, and then helping others achieve the same. I'm asking you to join me on that quest.

My hope for this book is that you and I can have a kitchen table conversation, and together, move farther down the road to where we want to be. My mission is to let you know that your best days don't have to be behind you. There is a purposeful life in front of you no matter what your circumstances are.

History is rife with stories of individuals who have overcome loss, pain, devastation, age, and financial calamity. In my book, I've included personal interviews with five people who conquered one loss after another to finally find a life, a purpose, and a mission for themselves.

A growing community of folks just like us realize that we have this one life, and we want to make the most of it. All you have to do is choose to join us—but it requires a total commitment. Let's jump into life together and turn the rest of our years into the best of our years. You've got what it takes, and these five pillars provide strategies for how to get unstuck and make the changes you need to live your life to the fullest.

You will also find questions at the end of each chapter and a place for you to answer the questions and make note of observations of your own. My intent with this book is to make this an interactive experience and not a lecture. This book is a plan that outlines a path for you to find your purpose and mission, but you have to choose to buy-in. I'm asking you to trust me, and my promise is that I will be here to help however I can.

PILLAR 1: COMPELLING VISION

SUE MARTIN

As Sue Martin steadied her finger on the rifle trigger, she simply wanted her life to end. She had had her fill of pain, loss, heartache, and struggle. She felt she had no more fight left, and she saw nothing to fight for.

Her life certainly hadn't begun this way. Her parents were her heroes and role models. She once had a dream of building a life like theirs, but as she sat alone in a friend's lake house, that dream seemed outside the realm of possibility. "I don't know why it was my parents' lives that I kept thinking about," Sue said. "On the surface, they had the perfect life. They had a house and two 'perfect' children, a boy and a girl. Daddy had a great job and Mama stayed home and raised those two 'perfect' children. I had none of that and no prospect of getting any of it."

Desperate and defeated, Sue pulled the trigger.

When she awoke in a pool of her own blood, Sue was thankful to be alive for the first time in a long time. In her memoir *Out of the Whirlpool*, Sue details her pain: "At that precise moment, at that precise and precious moment, I wanted to live." The spark of hope within her came as a surprise. "When I regained consciousness after eight hours, it was all dark. When the phone rang, and I heard a voice on the other end . . . someone had found me. Someone cared about me. A little spark of light was kindled in my soul, and I held onto it with all my might."

By her admission, Sue had an incredible childhood. She and her brother were adopted as infants into the family of a physician in Birmingham, Alabama. Sue's adopted family provided her with every privilege a child could imagine, including a loving father, a doting mother, and a brother as a best friend.

In many ways, Sue's childhood was idyllic. Her family was active in church and the community, and they took incredible vacations every summer, which allowed her to dive feet first into her love of horses. But somehow, somewhere, Sue got lost making the transition from the halcyon days of her childhood into adulthood. At the age of twenty-six, Sue found herself divorced, jobless, and living an existence that lacked any real direction. She was stuck and had no idea how to get out. "I don't know why," she said, "but I seemed to base my self-worth on what I had or hadn't accomplished. Those were all external things, bad breaks. And I can see now that those failures did not define me as a person. But from my point of view at the time, failure was all I could see."

It seemed everything Sue tried ended in failure. What's worse, with every stumble and setback, her passion and zest for life took a hit as well. With little confidence in herself or her future, and no hope that she could ever figure her way to a life of promise, she planned her death. But in doing so, she produced her resurrection.

Sue jokes that she was so bad at everything she couldn't even success-fully kill herself. Unfortunately, she did not escape injury. The shotgun had slipped from her hand and shifted ever so slightly, missing the most vital organs in her brain. While the gun didn't take her life, it did take her sight.

Fast forward forty years, where Sue not only survives but thrives. With grit and determination, a hallmark of her younger self, Sue refuses to use her blindness as an excuse for not living life to the fullest. On Facebook, she often posts pictures of herself hiking with her beautiful eight-year-old German Shepard, Quan, or cross-country skiing in Acadia National Park. She also shows herself gardening, cutting wood, or any number of activities you would never expect someone who is blind to engage in. As Sue said proudly, "I've taken back up almost everything I did before blindness."

Married and living in Maine with her husband Jim of more than thirty-five years, Sue has a life she loves, doing work she loves. Sue is currently a program and management analyst with the Veterans Affairs Office of Information and Technology. "One of the reasons I'm so passionate about the job I have right now," she said, "is because being blind has nothing to do with the job I'm doing." Sue finds great personal pride in having earned a job and found a career based on her talent and ability and not because of her disability.

Now, don't think the path from that cabin floor to her life today has been easy. Sue has undergone countless surgeries as well as intense physical rehabilitation and counseling sessions. She also has had to come to terms with living life as a blind person, but her spirit and courage have driven her to pursue all that life can be rather than dwell on what she has lost. With a second lease on life, Sue dove into building a life and career that fueled her. In doing so, she found a passion and a calling that today consumes her. Both were sparked by one of the first jobs she took after losing her sight, where she was just beginning to figure things out and find purpose in what she gives rather than what she gets.

"I took a job that was funded by a grant to provide service to our elders who were having vision problems," said Sue, "and that was a game-changer. For me, that's when serving became my passion. It was just so rewarding to walk in the door and meet a senior who thought, 'Oh my gosh, my vision is getting bad. I can't drive anymore. I can't do all the things I used to do,' and then give them not only the skills but also the attitude to get back on their feet and live the rich life they deserve. That's when serving really became my passion."

Sue is one of the most inspirational people you will ever meet. She exudes a love for life and lives every moment to its fullest, and in her memoir, she tells her inspiring story. As Sue looks back on her journey and what her suicide attempt, blindness, and the life she now lives have taught her, she no longer regrets what she has not accomplished, but recognizes all she has done. "Looking back," she said, "I can see how much courage, resilience, and determination it took to recreate myself and my life. I did what I had to do, and that was a lot."

When asked what advice she would give to someone struggling and hanging on by a thread, Sue settles on helping those losing hope. She encourages them to look deep within to see what she has had to learn for herself: that we've all got what it takes to beat whatever we're facing. According to Sue, "God gives us what we need when we need it. I just really firmly believe that when you're faced with a choice of challenging yourself or giving up, if you dig deep, you'll find what you need. It will be there."

Sue now has a vision for her life and future and is at peace with her past. "We never know what lies ahead, do we?" she said. "But because of where I once was, at rock bottom, and because of where I am now, a whole person, I have to believe that whatever lies ahead will be good. And if I get a lemon or two along the way, by golly, I'll make myself some lemonade!"

YOUR COMPELLING VISION

Though blind, Sue Martin lives out the first of The Five Pillars, compelling vision, which is the cornerstone of the other four pillars. Every other pillar or principle in the life you want builds off of a compelling vision. Frankly, if you feel lost and like you are just going through the motions, chances are good that you do not have a clear vision for your life.

The difficult thing about a vision is that it's hard to define and hard to find, but you certainly know when you've lost it because life is miserable and pointless, and you feel like you're walking around in a fog with no idea where you're headed or why. A quote from the incredible Helen Keller explains it well: "The only thing worse than being blind is having sight but no vision."

Your vision for your life has little to do with your ability to see, or your talent, skill, or gifts. It has more to do with what you can feel and know in your heart and soul. A compelling vision for your life comes by figuring out your 'why.'

Like so many of us, Sue Martin lost the vision for her life. You may currently feel like you've lost yours or you may have these kinds of self-sabotaging thoughts: "No one will miss me when I'm gone," or, "I'm a terrible husband (wife, son, daughter, parent, etc.)." You may even find yourself thinking, "My life is worthless." Those thoughts are all signs of someone who has lost a clear and compelling vision for their life—and they are all lies. Don't listen to them. They will keep you from finding your new why, or purpose, and your new compelling vision.

Remember: Without a clear vision, you are not being your most authentic self, and the unauthentic you is a voice you should never listen to.

On the Right Path

You've heard the phrase, "in the zone," right? Well, that's what happens when you are clear about why you are here, what you contribute, who you are, and better yet, who you are not. When you have a focused vision, your heart will be full, your mind will be active, and your spirit will be alive. With a clear map of where you are headed, you will arrive at your destination in the least amount of time. On the other hand, if your map is fuzzy and based on a guess, you may find yourself going in circles without knowing whether you are getting close or you may find yourself miles from where you need to be. Having a clear vision will keep you on the right path.

Off the Wrong Path

Having a clear and compelling vision also keeps you off the wrong path. Have you ever been in a job that is just okay, but you have this feeling that there's something better out there? Or maybe it's a relationship where you feel like you are settling, but you are afraid of being alone and wonder if this is the best you can get. Your heart sends you signals about what you really want, and you can ignore them or go with them.

Choosing a clear and compelling vision will cause you to become uncomfortable with settling for less than the best. Your standards for work, relationships, and health will also improve, and that's a good thing. But when you are off course and not living the clear and compelling vision you genuinely want for your life, there will be an irritating, nagging voice in your head or a feeling in the pit of your stomach, calling you to make a change and get back on course. Trust me. You won't find peace until you do. I've been there.

Port in a Storm

One other benefit of a clear and compelling vision is that it keeps you going when life gets tough. You will have bad days. Life happens and sometimes difficulty shows up on your doorstep. Loved ones die, jobs are lost, dreams don't work out as planned, and not all relationships work out. Having a clear vision will help you bounce back from the curves life throws at you.

Once you have a vision for your life, you will learn that it constantly grows and evolves as you grow and mature. A vision does not die with the loss of loved ones, dreams, jobs, or relationships. Until you draw your last breath, there will be a vision to pursue and a purpose to live for. If you woke up breathing today, consider it a green light to get to work on what you were put on this earth to do.

PILLAR TALK 1

At the end of each chapter, I will ask you questions. In some chapters, I will also give you action steps. Both will help you to think and reflect. Now, I am sure you would rather me lay out a plan for you to develop your life around these pillars, but I want you to arrive at the answers and insights yourself so that they work best for you. I have found that most folks are not finding the right answers for themselves because they aren't asking the right questions. The more time you spend meditating in quiet reflection, answering these questions, and trying these actions steps, the quicker and more accurately you will arrive at the right answers for your life.

Compelling Vision: Questions and Action Steps
1. When was the last time you felt happy, content, and proud of yourself?
2. What activity makes you lose track most of time?
3. Whose life, outlook, or success in life do you admire? Whom can you take to lunch this week?
4. What changes can you make to do more of how you answered questions 1 and 2?

Your Notes, Thoughts, Answers:

_____
_____
_____
_____
_____
_____
_____
_____
_____

It's my hope that the questions above will push you to go deep and wrestle with the answers until you have mined the gold and found the treasure. I have always found it helpful to do life with someone else, so I suggest finding someone who will read *The Five Pillars* with you and make this a group effort. Another piece of advice is to choose a partner with whom you can be open, transparent, and honest. In my life, that has usually meant someone in the friend zone and not a romantic relationship. But you do you, and I trust that you will find what works best.

One other thing: I can't state strongly enough how crucial it is to figure out your vision. The answers here may come slowly and even frustrate you at times, but don't give up. There is value in the struggle and toil that discovering your vision will bring. Once you get your compelling vision in place, you can begin developing a healthy lifestyle that adds the strength and stamina you need to live out your compelling life.

Your Notes, Thoughts, Answers:

_____
_____
_____
_____
_____
_____
_____

Lamb/5 Pillars

Lamb/5 Pillars

PILLAR 2: HEALTHY LIFESTYLE

MICHELLE STEINKE-BAUMGARD

Michelle Steinke-Baumgard received her wake-up call-in paradise. Accompanied by her husband Mitch on a scouting trip for her job as vice president of real estate for a private destination club, Michelle drew a line in the sandy beaches of Cabo San Lucas for her health. She had a six-figure job, a husband who loved her, and two adorable young kids. What Michelle didn't have was good health or a positive self-image. She didn't like who she saw in photos and felt limited by her weight. The call Michelle answered in Cabo had been nagging her for many years.

"Before Cabo," Michelle said, "I'd been on and off again with fitness for years. Once I became a mom and busy corporate VP, it all went downhill, and I just wasn't very good at sticking with it consistently. I was pretty fit in high school but [I] had really stopped taking care of myself for years."

It was while she was on the trip with Mitch that something within her hit critical mass. The time to change was now or never.

"I was miserable," she said. "He wanted to go do all these fun things. He wanted to go dune buggy, and he wanted to do things on the beach. And I just didn't feel like doing any of it. I was overworked, exhausted, and really disappointed in myself, so I kind of made a decision right there in Cabo. Enough."

After returning home, Michelle went to work on herself. "I got involved with the gym, and I just went hard and heavy into it like I never had before. My workouts were typically earlier in the day, and I mostly lifted weights and did HIIT-style training. I cleaned up my diet considerably and moved to a largely whole-food-based diet, and I immediately, within a couple of weeks, could see the difference in my attitude, my mood, and my energy level. My work production was better, and I was a far better wife and mother."

In six short weeks, Michelle was beginning to see the results of her hard work and commitment, but then she received word that Mitch had been in a tragic accident. "I was at my daughter's dance class," she said. "He was supposed to meet us to watch her. First time he was ever going to see her dance. She was two. I got the phone call that there had been a crash, and I knew immediately."

On October 9, 2009, the plane Mitch piloted crashed shortly after takeoff. In an instant, Michelle was a widow and single mother. "The shock [was] extreme, and I often didn't even feel like I was living in reality," she said. "Your entire world is turned upside down."

What Michelle did just days later, surprised even her. She returned to the gym. "The ironic thing is I quit fitness programs I can't tell you how many times. Any excuse was a reason to quit," she explained, "I can't quit, " she thought, "it was too important.

If Michelle's first wake-up call was at a beautiful tropical location, her second was in the midst of tragedy. Loss has a powerful way of separating hope from hype, and what matters in life from what doesn't. For Michelle, her health and well-being had become a priority, as she describes it here: "I just knew it was something I had to do for myself, for my children, and for Mitch's legacy. Death gives clarity, and I realized in a moment just how important my own life and my own health was when he died. I was all my children had, and I needed to be strong, fit, and healthy for the road ahead."

So, with a drive and commitment that bordered on obsession, Michelle poured herself into becoming the best version of herself. While wounds from the loss and heartache slowly healed, the gym became her sanctuary. "I always tell people it saved my life," she said, "and I don't say that lightly. My kids were one and two, so I could go to the gym and completely escape being a mother, a solo mother, being the town widow, all these things. For one hour, I just went hard at my workout. I'd sometimes sweat and cry at the same time."

Michelle's commitment to a healthy lifestyle renewed her mind and reshaped her health. In all, she lost seventy pounds and found a renewed purpose.

Today, Michelle is remarried and lives an adventurous life as an entrepreneur and philanthropist, helping others pursue their dreams, bucket lists, and health goals. She also helps people move forward when faced with heartache, loss, and hardship so they can live a full life despite the circumstances they find themselves in. Michelle has written an incredible book about her journey called *Healthy Healing*.

When Michelle looks back on her life and the loss and pain she has endured, her mind settles on the gift of exercise.

"It became nonnegotiable in my life," she said. "What I did is I sat down, and I realized how different my life looked in that six weeks or whatever it was from when I started, and I realized that it gave me so many benefits that aren't tangible. It's the energy, it's the mood, it's the way you carry your shoulders and the way you walk through life. And that became very nonnegotiable for me. I think the other thing for me was I had two babies, and I wanted to lead by example. I wanted to show them that our lives still mattered, even if he wasn't here. And for me, that started with taking care of myself."

YOUR HEALTHY LIFESTYLE

The second pillar to living the life of your dreams is to have a healthy lifestyle. Once you get clear on your vision, you will need a vehicle to get you there. We are all renting space in the only option we've got, and despite the way some of us treat our bodies, we only get one. There are no do-overs, so you would be wise to treat your body like a prized possession. As Michelle found, becoming your best self requires an investment in your health and wellness.

In each of The Five Pillars presented in this book, you will find the theme, "Why settle?". If something is worth doing, it's worth doing well, and that is particularly true when it comes to taking care of your body.

I see three major reasons why a healthy lifestyle is an essential pillar of the life you want to live.

The Body Is a Wonderland

Why do we so often push our bodies to the limit to see how much punishment they can take? It's like we are given the keys to a beautiful Ferrari, then we go and fill it with low octane fuel and wonder why it doesn't run well, or we get mad when it breaks down completely.

I challenge you to change your mindset when it comes to your body instead of seeing what kinds of junk you can fill it with and do the minimum to keep it on the road. Why don't you find out once and for all what your body is truly capable of? How strong, fit, healthy, and energized can you get?

You only get one body, so why not cherish it?

What's Good for the Body Is Good for the Mind

A healthy lifestyle is critical to living your best life. It's great for your body and equally great for your mind. For Michelle, the gym became the place she would go to get away from all the stress and sadness, and she would leave renewed and refueled. What Michelle discovered is also backed up by research, and the science is clear: strength training and aerobic exercise have multiple effects on much more than just your waistline, including preventing cognitive decline, reducing anxiety and stress, serving as an antidepressant, boosting IQ, improving learning and memory, increasing creativity, and more.

My brother Mike struggled with depression. Millions of others, including myself, struggle with it, too. When things don't go our way, it's easy to indulge in comfort food and begin a downward spiral that is hard to get out of. If you do nothing else but focus on your health, you will be shocked at how it will affect every other area of your life. It will boost your mood, which might shake you out of a rut.

Look Good, Feel Good, Live Good

Another benefit of a healthy lifestyle is the boost in self-confidence. Endorphins are the brain's feel-good neurotransmitters that help build confidence. Runners activate endorphins producing what's called "the runners high," but did you know that aerobic activity, like a game of tennis or a simple hike, can activate them as well? There's just something uplifting about getting a workout logged and over with for the day. The sense of accomplishment and pride is addictive and will help you be and feel better than you have in a long time.

Being your best self means being able to do what you need to do when you need to do it—and do it with focus, energy, and stamina. That only happens when you have a body that can handle it. Adopting a healthy lifestyle will provide you with a dependable vehicle to get you where you want to go. Failing to do so will find you limping across the finish line or, worse yet, never reaching it. You're better than that, so make the changes today to get fit, healthy, and strong. Turn your body into a peak performer and become the best version of yourself.

Before I get to the questions for Pillar 2, here's one final thought. On airplanes, flight attendants read the following preflight safety instructions:

"In the event of a sudden loss of cabin pressure, oxygen masks will automatically descend from the ceiling. Grab the mask and pull it over your face. If you have a child traveling with you, secure your mask before assisting with theirs."

Why do they instruct you to put on your mask before helping someone else? Because at full capacity, you will do a better job of helping others. You will have a clearer head and be at 100 percent. The same is true when you take care of your body. You will never be at your best or able to give it your all if you are not at your physical best. When you run, do yoga, lift weights, or choose fruits and vegetables over a burger and fries, you are essentially putting on your oxygen mask. You become not only good for you, but also good for everyone around you.

PILLAR TALK 2

Before you start working on the questions and action steps for a healthy lifestyle, quickly review your last assignment for Pillar 1. How are you doing with getting a clear picture of a compelling vision for your life? Remember: Every pillar builds off of a compelling vision, so you want to devote the necessary time and effort to figure it out. There's no rush, despite the anxiety you may be feeling to get something down on paper and move on. If it's worth doing, it's worth doing right. So flip back to the questions for Pillar 1 and review your answers. Then come back to Pillar 2 and start on the activities below to help you secure a healthy lifestyle.

Healthy Lifestyle: Questions and Action Steps

1. Where are you physically? Make an appointment with your doctor to assess where you are and where you are headed if you don't make some changes.
2. Based on the data you receive from your doctor visit, what are some specific goals for your weight loss and health? Are there any markers that concern your doctor, such as glucose levels, cholesterol, blood pressure, etc.?
3. What changes will you make to your diet? Do you have a goal weight you want to reach and a timetable to get there? Diet is the secret to a healthy lifestyle. What you eat either gives you life or kills you, so become a student and start making wise decisions.
4. What are your fitness plans? Write down your plans for increasing activity and movement. Are you going to lift weights or go to spin class? Write it all down so you can see it. Put it on your calendar.

Remember: A goal without a plan is just a wish. Set some goals and deadlines, and don't be afraid to step up your game. You don't have time to waste. Now is the time to start. Once you have completed Pillars 1 and 2, you'll be ready to begin Pillar 3, where you will find out how to build a life filled with rich relationships.

Your Notes, Thoughts, Answers:

_____
_____
_____
_____
_____
_____
_____
_____
_____
_____
_____
_____
_____
_____
_____
_____
_____

Lamb/5 Pillars

PILLAR 3: RICH RELATIONSHIPS

BILLY BAKER

The email's subject line was nothing special: "We have a story you'll be perfect for." As a reporter for *The Boston Globe*, Billy Baker got similar pitches from his editor every week. Unable to wriggle his way out of the story he did not want to tell, Billy was assigned rather than asked to write a feature on why so many middle-aged men had few, if any, friends.

"When I was called to the editor's office," Billy said, "the editor rattle[ed] off all these dire health statistics, which was his point for the story. Like we need to find a way to get out there all these dire stats about how much more likely you are to die or whatever if you're lonely."

As his editor made a case for Billy to write the story, the idea started to hit Billy differently. He explained it to me from his home outside of Boston in a way that felt personal.

"If it's true that friendship is really the key to a happy, healthy, long life, and loneliness is this epidemic, then I want to hack my life to get these benefits. And so, when I took on the assignment, I think it was partly like I wanted to learn the science so I could help myself."

When Billy took on the assignment to write the column, he was a young dad and husband in his early 40s with two young boys and a home in the suburbs. Billy realized that he wasn't too far removed from the subjects in the startling studies that had given birth to the idea for the story he was about to write. So he went to work doing what he's done hundreds of times in his career. He gathered information, researched, wrote, and submitted the story.

The article, "The Biggest Threat Facing middle-aged Men Isn't Smoking or Obesity. It's loneliness," ran in the *Globe Magazine* on March 9, 2017. What happened next was the last thing Billy had anticipated. The story he was hesitant to take on hit a nerve and went viral. It became the most popular story the *Globe* had ever published at the time and was read by more than a million people. Thousands of emails began filling Billy's inbox from, as Billy described, "men and women, young and old, sharing what worked, what had failed, and mostly thanking me for giving them the kick in the ass to get back with their friends."

Multiple emails came from agents, too. They wanted Billy to turn his column into a book, and in 2021, he added the title of 'author' to his resume when *We Need to Hang Out* was released by Simon & Schuster.

In his book, Billy makes the case that loneliness is a killer and a serious public health threat. One study he cites is the work of Dr. Richard S. Schwartz, a Cambridge psychiatrist who studies the health toll of loneliness. Schwartz found that loneliness can be as much of a long-term risk factor as smoking. Billy also cites a Brigham Young University study from 2015 that collected data from 3.5 million people over a thirty-five-year span and found that being lonely, isolated, or living on your own raises the risk of premature death by 26-32 percent.

After providing a sobering wake-up call, Billy offers this advice: "If you don't have active membership in a tribe, you have to find one, or you need to create one." Billy also suggests that the clearest path to creating new friendships is in shared interests like running, cycling, bowling, or a book club. He cites 'velvet hooks' as shared passions or interests that naturally and easily connect us and give reasons for consistently getting together. A classic velvet hook is two gearheads getting together to restore an old car or book lovers gathering over coffee and snacks for book club.

In his article and book, Billy makes a passionate and convincing case for the value of connection and friendship. After doing a deep dive into loneliness and the power of friendship, he offers two parting pieces of advice: "If you don't want to see your doctor, then see your friends and also call a friend. And do it now. Your life and health will be better for it."

CREATING RICH RELATIONSHIPS

The third of The Five Pillars that make up a life of meaning, purpose, and impact is rich relationships. If you are clear about your vision and in the best health of your life, but you are blowing it in creating rich relationships, you will never be at peace. You will be distracted while pursuing all you were placed on this earth to do.

Billy Baker's original article for *The Boston Globe* and his ensuing book, *We Need to Hang Out: A Memoir of Making Friends,* got such immediate and powerful reactions because most of us are awful at relationships. So fill your life with people who give you joy, love, laughter, and encouragement, as they are essential to the life you want to live.

Some sage advice says, "If possible, live at peace with everyone." Can we all agree that peaceful relationships make life so much easier and high-drama relationships are exhausting? Life is full of enough hills and valleys and tests and trials for you to add relational drama and chaos. Conversely, if you have people you love and know who love you—people pulling for you and in your corner—life will be more enjoyable and fulfilling.

This section on relationships is the longest in this book because relationships are complicated—and relationships are complicated because people are complex. Relationships have an ebb and flow. They are not static.

It's helpful to view tending to the relationships in your life as tending to a garden. Before you plant the first seed, you must prepare the soil, remove the weeds, and clear it for planting. By taking the time to remove anything that will hinder your goal for a healthy garden, you ensure its success in producing healthy, vibrant, beautiful green fruits and vegetables to enjoy. The same is needed to prepare your life for relational success. You've got to remove toxic connections to make way for healthy relationships.

So, let's get to the three reasons why I say rich relationships are an essential pillar in the life you aspire to live.

Toxic Cleanse

Relational guilt, shame, and regret are unnecessary hurdles to the life you want to live. If you hear someone's name and immediately feel anger, shame, guilt, regret, bitterness, or the flash of any other negative emotion, it's a sign that something is wrong, and you'd be wise not to ignore it. You've probably heard the saying that bitterness is like consuming poison and expecting it to kill someone else; well, those unresolved emotions are killers, too. Listen to this old guy, here. It's time to deal with them. Life is too short to have a bunch of garbage between you and someone important to you. Before you dismiss them as unimportant, remember: If they were unimportant, you wouldn't be spending so much time thinking about them.

I learned this lesson at the age of seventeen when working on a job site with my father. He had a massive heart attack and was gone in an instant. There was no chance to say goodbye. Sadly, his relationships with my mom, my siblings, his siblings, and his friends were where they would stay for eternity. This truth is a big one, and it's hard and tough to reconcile. It may even be difficult for you to think about, but believe me, it's time to do all you can to live peaceably with everyone.

Life-Giving Relationships

Life-giving relationships make the highs higher and the lows easier. If you make The Five Pillars a formula that you follow, you will achieve success like you never have. Having someone to share the ride with is incredible. Being able to say, "We did it," is one of life's greatest joys and achievements. If you say that into a mirror because you have a stream of cast-aside relationships, the top will not nearly be as sweet. Who wants to be alone at the top anyway?

As sweet as it will be once you get to the top, the journey won't be all sunshine and rainbows. Any journey worth taking will have its share of struggle, heartache, and challenge. Having someone who you know is in your corner and there when you call will massively increase your chances of success. To have such a relationship takes investment on your part and only comes from the time you have put into it. As the saying goes, be the kind of friend you want to have. A friend who is dependable, encouraging, wise, and honest will invite friends who are the same.

Although being a good friend is a sure way to make and keep friends, investing in life-giving relationships is not something that will happen overnight or without intention. As Billy suggested, this may require you to take charge and put yourself out there in a way that makes you feel vulnerable and even awkward. But having a healthy circle of friends is vital to the life we all want to live, so call that friend you lost contact with; join a book club, soccer league, or church group. If you can't find a group that interests you, maybe you need to start one. The days of living in the shadows and sidelines are over. It's time to pursue the life you want and surround yourself with the kind of community you want to be a part of.

Intentionality

    Being honest and intentional when it comes to your romantic and platonic relationships is vital to the life you are building. The sobering reality is that you will never be able to fully commit your heart to any person or endeavor if a piece of you is held hostage by feelings like guilt, shame, bitterness, or regret. To get where you want to go will take an all-in commitment to proactively do the work necessary to find relational health and peace. If your head, heart, and soul cannot fully commit, you will not be able to give your best, and that's just not good enough.

    Where you are headed, you need a clear mind and heart, or your emotional baggage will keep you from where you want your relationships to go. Doing the work to make things right in your key relationships will give you a feeling of peace and freedom, allowing you to develop relationships faster than ever before. You will be like a prisoner set free—because that's what you are. You're free of the burdens and weights you once carried, but you must take charge and be intentional about fixing what's broken and getting this right.

Do All You Can Do, Then Let It Go

Let's revisit the sage advice shared in the third paragraph of this section: "If possible, live at peace with everyone." Relationships can get messy and difficult, and they are not easily repaired. I get that. In fact, you will run into people who have no interest in repairing their relationship with you. That hurts, and it's painful, but it's reality—and you simply cannot control another human being. They are their own people and are not required to accept your apology or invitation to get together for coffee. That's okay. You do you. You take the high road and accept responsibility for your actions and the hurt you have caused, but don't take on the burden of how someone else receives it. You can only do what you can do. You do your best and try to make good. Sometimes, that's all you can do—and sometimes, it takes a long, long time. That's okay, just as long as you "make an effort" to live peaceably with everyone.

Your Notes, Thoughts, Answers:

_____

_____

_____

_____

_____

_____

_____

Lamb/5 Pillars

Lamb/5 Pillars

PILLAR TALK 3

How did your review of Pillar 1 go? Have you completed the questions and action steps for Pillar 2? Have you discovered any connections between them? It's important for you to make progress with the pillars of vision and healthy lifestyle before starting on the questions and action steps for Pillar 3, rich relationships. Once you start working on the Pillar 3 activities, keep the following information in mind as you begin.

Some of the most challenging work you will do in your life is on relationships. Investing in people can be messy and heartbreaking at times, but finding your tribe and developing relationships with those who fill your heart with unconditional love and acceptance will add a quality to your life that is well worth the time and investment.

As you grow, you may need to revisit the answers and insights you've come up with for each pillar and tweak them. That is perfectly fine. My vision for my life has gone through several iterations as I have changed. Discoveries written on paper are not etched in stone. So, look back over your thoughts to the questions and insights from the action steps in previous chapters, and make sure they are helping you progress toward firmly placing each pillar for the life you are building.

When you've finished your review, come back to Pillar 3 and work on answering the questions that will help you develop rich relationships.

Rich Relationships: Questions and Action Steps:
1. Is there anyone who causes you to feel guilt, shame, bitterness, and regret when you hear their name? If so, write down those names today.
2. Is it possible to contact any or all of them?
3. Is there anyone's name that elicits a positive reaction like a pleasant memory or simply hearing their name brings a smile to your face or fills you with joy? If so, write down those names.
4. Who can you contact today? Choose the most appropriate means, be it by email, phone, text, or letter. Don't rush in. Give this some thought. Don't let the fear of opening old wounds or a difficult conversation allow you to ignore this section. Lay out a plan, however long it takes, and work the plan. Your life will be better for it. Be brave, be kind, be full of grace, and be patient.

Your Notes, Thoughts, Answers:

_____
_____
_____
_____
_____
_____

Lamb/5 Pillars

Fantastic! You've worked on getting your relationships on track. Now it's time to turn your focus on the workplace, where you will likely spend more waking hours than anywhere else. Time to dive into Pillar 4 and learn what it takes to build a fulfilling career.

PILLAR 4: FULFILLING CAREER
CAROL GARDNER

The divorce papers signed, Carol Gardner and her attorney sat in silence. Carol had heard that psychologists rate divorce just below the death of a loved one in terms of stressful life experiences. As she sat in a stunned silence in her attorney's office in downtown Portland, Oregon, Carol could not imagine anything being more painful than what she was feeling. "Sweetheart," Carol's attorney began, getting up to walk Carol out of her office, "you need to either get a therapist or a dog."

"It was heartbreaking," Carol told me. "I was 52, divorced, broke, and depressed."

So, Carol followed her attorney's advice and got the dog she had always wanted—a bulldog. She named her four-month-old pup Zelda.

As if the divorce wasn't painful enough, Carol and her now ex-husband had a million dollars in debt from a failed business that had to be paid. "I needed to make money," she said. "My debt was enormous, so I had to make money in a hurry."

An entrepreneur since childhood, Carol had done well as a creative director in advertising campaigns for some huge corporations. Facing a sizable debt as a single mother with a young son at home, Carol didn't have time to complain about her lot in life, so she went to work.

A friend had told her about a contest at her local pet shop. The prize was free dog food. The contest got her entrepreneurial and creative juices flowing, and she recruited Zelda to help. Carol snapped a photo of her cute, wrinkly little pooch in a bubble bath wearing a Santa hat and captioned the card, "For Christmas, I got a dog for my husband . . . good trade, huh?"

The reaction to the card was more than Carol could have ever imagined. She not only won the contest, but she also won a contract that would erase her debt and make her millions. "Someone made a connection for me with a company called Westland Giftware. And Westland no longer exists because they made so much money they don't need to work anymore," Carol said, with her trademark humor.

As Carol produced photo shoots of Zelda in hundreds of different outfits, she came up with witty sayings that Westland put on greeting cards. Within six months, Zelda Wisdom greeting cards took off, and Carol's debt problem was solved. "They did Zelda everything," she said. "They did figurines. They did snow globes. They did magnets. They did cookie jars. They did banks. They did notebooks. They did everything, and Zelda made them millions of dollars, so it was a good connection."

Today, some twenty-five years later, Zelda Wisdom is an established global brand with yearly sales in the high seven figures. Carol Gardner is still a ball of energy and going strong, spreading a message of grit, hope, and resilience through bulldogs that inspire and encourage millions every year.

And Carol certainly has hung on, both in business and in life. She is proud of her relationship with her ex-husband and the friendship they now have. "We are best friends. We really are. We talk every day."

Creating Zelda figurines that read, "Tough times don't last, but tough people do," is Carol's way of passionately sharing her advice with those currently going through a difficult time in their life or business. "When you think about that," she said, referring to the figurine, "and when I say that to people who are going through a tough time, I want them to think they're tougher than that."

Carol is plenty tough, and her never-give-up attitude has served her well. While it would have been easier to quit when life dealt her a painful blow, she found the strength to turn her pain into joy and spread her unique brand of creativity and humor around the world, touching countless lives. In doing so, she found her life's work.

These days, Carol often finds herself quizzed on her secrets to success, and she shares her successful entrepreneurial formula.

"If you're going to come up with an idea, it has to be three things. It has to be daring. It has to be different. Those are the two easy things. The hard part is it has to be smart. And that's my whole formula for entrepreneurship."

Daring, different, and smart. Three words that would also describe Carol Gardner because she dared to get up when she was knocked down. Carol is also different enough not to accept defeat, and her smarts, creativity—and a bulldog—helped her build a true American success story.

FINDING YOUR FULFILLING CAREER

You've probably heard this quote attributed to Confucius: "Choose a job you love, and you will never work a day in your life again." Most of us can agree on the negative aspect of the quote's inverse. If you are stuck in a job you hate, few things are more miserable. The positive aspect is that if you are doing what you love, time flies, your heart swells, and your mind is alive. It is a beautiful thing and an experience for all to enjoy.

However, you will never find the job you love until you get certain of what you are looking for, and I want to try and help you discover it.

As a big fan of formulas and processes, I believe that if there's a tried-and-true pattern that has worked many times throughout the centuries, then it's worth paying attention to. The formula to find the job of your dreams is apparent in the paths of thousands who have found it for themselves.

Here's the formula: Passion + Talent + Market Need = A Fulfilling Career

Lead With Passion

The first step to finding a fulfilling and meaningful career is identifying an area of passion. One-third of our lives are spent working at a job, so spending that time doing something you find joy and are passionate about is a must. A bad boss, low pay, and difficult coworkers all come with building a career. Life is full of seasons, and a tough, challenging season at a place of employment can be doubly miserable if you hate your job. On the other hand, the tough days will be much more manageable and easier to endure if you work in an area that brings you joy, excites your curiosity and creativity, and interests you.

A good way to discover what you're passionate about is to pay attention to what you are naturally drawn to. Is there a subject matter you are attracted to in books, magazines, documentaries, or individuals? In my free time, I always read about human performance, leadership, and how the super successful or talented have achieved great things. For you, what would it be? Is there a theme or common thread you are drawn to?

Second Nature

The second step in finding a fulfilling career is to find your talent. What comes naturally to you, is easy for you, or feels like second nature? You want to find a career that feels more like a calling and something that you have the talent and ability to be great at.

Michael Jordan is considered the greatest basketball player of all time. He was born with the size and skill for the sport and was raised by a family that valued work ethic and commitment. Plenty of other basketball players were also tall and had a great work ethic, but what separated Jordan from the others was that he was poetry in motion with a basketball in his hands. Jordan only became the greatest because he got the most out of his natural gift by working hard.

Find a career that pushes you to break boundaries and gives you the opportunity to soar like Michael Jordan. Your ability to excel at something you have a gift and aptitude for will make your trek to the top much easier. Conversely, trying to reach the top at a career you are not naturally gifted in will leave you feeling like you are swimming in quicksand.

What's something that comes to you so easily that you are surprised when you receive compliments on it? What do you do that doesn't really feel like work or take much effort? Maybe you pick up something quicker than others. Another possible clue is a class or subject in school that others struggled with, but you passed with great ease.

Market Demand

The third step to finding a career you enjoy is seeing where the answers to steps one and two intersect with a market need. I am a big dreamer and believe in following your heart and engaging in things you are passionate about. I am also a realist and a sober thinker. It is a waste of time to have a big dream and a naive understanding of how the real-world works, so the third and final component to the formula for a fulfilling career cannot be ignored or overlooked.

Look for where your passion and talent intersect with something people are looking for. Have you met someone who has a job that stirs something within you and piques your interest? Since life comes with a price tag and we have to pay rent, college loans, and a car note, we've got to earn a living with financial rewards. Therefore, doing something that someone wants to pay you well for is vital.

A tough-love sort of warning here: you need to look at this with brutal honesty. If there is no market for where your passion and talent intersect, you need to call that a hobby and keep looking. All three components have to add up. If they don't, keep searching.

Your Notes, Thoughts, Answers:

_____

_____

_____

_____

_____

_____

_____

_____

_____

_____

Lamb/5 Pillars

PILLAR TALK 4

Let's once again stop and review. By now, you should have begun or hopefully completed the work necessary to get an accurate read on the first three pillars.

> ~ Your vision should be taking shape.
>
> ~ You should be adopting the necessary. changes for a healthy lifestyle and started seeing and feeling the difference.
>
> ~ You should be noticing some obvious changes you need to make regarding those who will and will not be a part of your life moving forward.

I encourage you to stay the course. Anytime you make changes, it's difficult, but you are building something that will make the rest of your years the best of your years. The investment of the few weeks it will take you to put The Five Pillars into action will pay off for the rest of your life. You are investing in you. You are betting on yourself and your future. Don't give up, and don't turn back now. You've come too far. You've got this!

Ready to tackle the questions and action steps for Pillar 4 that will land your dream job? Let's go.

Fulfilling Career: Questions and Action Steps

1. What are you passionate about? What do you dream about or read about in your free time and find yourself fantasizing about doing one day?

2. What are your natural gifts and talents? What do you get complimented on that requires little to no effort?
3. Where do the answers to questions one and two intersect in the marketplace? Make a list of jobs that call for or require someone with your passion and talent.
4. What can you do today to map out a plan to get from the job you have to the job you want? Chart out a course that begins today, right where you are, without having to quit your job. Begin with a plan requiring small, reasonable, and responsible steps that make your dream a reality.

Your Notes, Thoughts, Answers:

_____
_____
_____
_____
_____
_____
_____
_____

Lamb/5 Pillars

Lamb/5 Pillars

Finding the right career takes some trial and error. Don't be too proud to admit to yourself or your Five-Pillars partner when you mess up or make a wrong turn. If you have a job that is not the right fit for you, own it and plan your next best move. Taking a step back and charting your career choices may reveal some motivations or clues for what to clean up before you are ready to find the right fit.

Our choices in life often reveal insecurities and fears that rise to the surface and devour our hopes and dreams for the sake of safety and security. These pitfalls are all great conversation starters for you and your Five-Pillars partner. Keep them in mind as you move on to the fifth and final pillar, Big mission. It's the one that brings the most joy.

Your Notes, Thoughts, Answers:

_____
_____
_____
_____
_____
_____
_____
_____
_____
_____

Lamb/5 Pillars

PILLAR 5: BIG MISSION
RODNEY SMITH

Alone in his apartment, Rodney Smith didn't get it. His parents had sent him from his home in Bermuda to school in the U.S. to find his place and purpose. Instead, he felt more alone and lost than ever. With the walls of his apartment closing in around him, a desperate Rodney cried out to God, "Use me, somehow, some way. Use me for good."

Rodney felt like an outsider from the moment his parents sent him to a boarding school in upstate New York to address a learning disability. He had always felt different, and in school, he found it especially difficult to pronounce some words, eliciting chuckles from other students when he struggled to read aloud. "I couldn't read some spelling words or read a book," Rodney told me. "It was hard."

While struggling to find his way, Rodney found strength in his mother's steadfast faith and belief. "She always encouraged me," he said. "She never gave up. And as long as you have that one person who believes in you, you can do it."

Rodney ultimately made his way to Alabama A&M University in Huntsville to pursue a computer science degree. It was in Huntsville, on the way to class, that Rodney's prayer was answered in the most unlikely of ways. "I came across an elderly man mowing his lawn," he said.

"It looked like he was struggling, and that's when I pulled over and helped him out. And that act of kindness would change my life forever."

As Rodney got back in his car and resumed his trek to campus, his mind drifted back to that prayer years earlier at the lowest point of his life. His desire to be used for good had been answered, but in a simple act of helping that elderly man, Mr. Brown, his neighbor in need, Rodney's mission was born. "That night, I went home and made a post on Facebook saying if anyone knows anyone, either a single parent or a veteran who needs their lawn mowed, please let me know."

From that single Facebook post grew a nonprofit business that used mowing yards to teach young people responsibility and the power of kindness and generosity. Rodney issued a fifty-yard challenge that would recruit young people to mow fifty yards for free with the promise of a new lawnmower, weed eater, and leaf blower once the challenge was complete.

Today the fifty-yard challenge has been accepted by more than 3,000 kids who have mowed more than 21,000 lawns in all fifty states and eight foreign countries. Rodney's dream of being used for good has been answered thousands of times, and the impact he has had on countless lives surprises even him.

This young outsider from Bermuda with a learning disability has shared his story on ABC, CBS, NBC, CNN, Fox News, The Today Show, and Good Morning America. Even so, Rodney finds the greatest joy in seeing his organization help veterans, single moms, or the elderly every day. "Oh man, it's good helping someone," Rodney said, "especially someone you see that needs the help. Imagine ... there's so many more people just like Mr. Brown around this country."

Grateful to have found his mission, Rodney knows the world is full of folks still searching for their unique way to contribute, give back, and make a difference.

"A lot of people pass on without finding their purpose," he said. "Imagine all the ideas that pass away before people find their purpose. God has given you that idea. You just have to take that chance."

If you are struggling to find your purpose and a mission that excites and inspires you, consider taking Rodney's advice: "Find what you're good at, find what you love, or just ask God what He wants you to do, and He will show you—and then just do it."

YOUR BIG MISSION

Up to this point, I've written *The Five Pillars* mainly about you and a little about me. However, this fifth and final pillar is all about others because the fifth pillar in a life of purpose, passion, and legacy requires a bigger mission than you or me.

One of life's great truths is that you will never feel satisfied, fulfilled, or happy by what you get in life but only by what you give. I know that is counterintuitive and goes against so much of what we think, feel, and hear all around us, but it's a fact. Choosing a mission bigger than yourself in which you to invest your time, energy, and resources will satisfy a desire that you may not even know you have.

Focus on Others

Giving to others through a mission that you are committed to will divert your focus off your problems. When you are stuck in an important area of your life like relationships, career, or even health, you can become consumed by it. Let's take careers: if you hate your job and have to drag yourself to work every day, it's nearly impossible to see the good in it. All you see are the tasks you hate, the mean boss, or the embarrassing pay. That's only made worse by your younger sibling or that classmate from high school who has a wonderful job making incredible money and flying all around the world while you are stuck in what feels like another dead-end job.

Relax. What you are seeing is not reality. I would bet your job is not as bad as you think, and their jobs are not as good as you think. That's the problem with being self-consumed. You know your situation inside and out, but you only see the parts of their jobs that they want you to see. Having a mission that takes your focus off you and puts it onto someone else improves your perspective.

Attitude of Gratitude

A mission also develops a grateful heart. You truly don't know how good you have it until you walk in the shoes of someone who has it worse than you. Furthermore, you don't realize all you have to give because you only see your shortcomings and deficiencies. I promise you that someone out there can use your help. Whether you serve in a soup kitchen, teach English as a second language, cut someone's grass, or work in the church nursery, there are needs all around you. If you can't see them, you aren't looking, and the reason you aren't looking is that you are focused only on yourself and your problems.

Legacy

The third and final reason why having a mission matter is that it allows you to make an impact that will outlive you. Have you heard that old adage about the best time to plant a tree? The best time to plant a tree was twenty years ago, and the second-best time is now. We all have to start doing a better job of taking care of each other and taking ownership of how to make our little slices of the world better. As good as your community might be, it will only be better once you show up in full. You bring something unique that no one else can bring, so show up. You may be surprised at how fulfilling it will be.

I have learned the benefits of showing up firsthand. My wife and I bought a couple of restaurant franchises a few years ago to invest in our financial future. Without question, the most valuable outcome of our time in the restaurant business has been the opportunity to invest in the lives of our employees. We have had many high school and college student employees, some of whom this was their first job. The gift of helping them learn how to work, get into college, and grow as people has been so much more satisfying and rewarding than any other aspect of owning a restaurant.

I had no idea I would love this as much as I do. To be honest, I went into it as more of a financial investment. The financial reward pales in comparison to the reward of getting a text or email from an employee when they get accepted into the college of their dreams or when I run into one of their parents and they thank me, with tears in their eyes, for the way we have invested in their child's future. You can't put a price on it.

That's the way a mission works. It's not about you or me; it's about what we can do to help someone else. Like the amazing Dr. Martin Luther King, Jr. said: "Life's most persistent and urgent question is, 'What are you doing for others?'" It's a question that having a Big Mission answers.

Your Notes, Thoughts, Answers:

___
___
___
___
___
___
___
___
___

Lamb/5 Pillars

Lamb/5 Pillars

PILLAR TALK 5

Finding a Big Mission is one of the most intuitive endeavors in this book, but we often behave like pinballs bouncing through life. We are so busy that not only do we fail to stop and smell the roses, but we are also oblivious to their existence. Our lives are sometimes filled with painful moments that leave gaping holes, deep regret, and shameful thoughts that stay with us, but a mission allows us to turn those unfocused moments and tough losses into big wins. My mission is writing this book to help people get unstuck and find their way to happiness and wholeness; but it is born out of the loss of one of my favorite people ever— my brother Mike.

So, as you answer the questions and follow the action steps for Pillar 5, once again, don't be afraid to be open and honest with your Five-Pillars partner and yourself. There is too much good work on this Earth for you to do, and you are uniquely qualified to do it. Often that requires turning the ashes of your former self into a beautiful person who helps others.

Big Mission: Questions and Action Steps

Take some time to review your answers and insights from Pillars 1–4. Notice any correlations? See if you can find any links between Pillar 5 and the others.

1. What charity or philanthropic endeavor connects with your heart? When you hear about an event coming up or see something on the news or in the newspaper about a certain

fundraiser, which ones cause you to pause and pay attention?
2. Is there a charity that connects with your history, such as a cause that helps something you've gone through? For me, it's the American Heart Association. My dad died of a heart attack when he was just forty-eight. My brother Mike died of heart-related issues as well. When I invest my time and money into this issue, it connects me with their memory. Try to find what does that for you.
3. Make a list of charities or causes that you would be interested in helping.
4. Narrow the list of your top two or three and take the time to visit the organizations over the next week or two. Spend a day meeting the leadership to see what they actually do. See if your head and heart connect with these groups and if you are confident in get behind them.

Once you have worked through the Pillar 5 questions, take a moment to see how your plan is coming together. While I am a big fan of thought and deliberation, my goal is to get you to arrive at an action plan. At this point, you should see the results of your work taking shape in action plans for every pillar.

Lamb/5 Pillars

Your Notes, Thoughts, Answers:

_____

_____

_____

_____

_____

_____

There's a time to discuss, a time to get things done, and a time to live an incredible life out there, so keep your eyes on the life that awaits who you are becoming. You don't have time to waste allowing pesky, self-defeating thoughts to hound you anymore. They are like insects, and it's time to stomp them out. They can be devastating, and they are not welcome in you because you are becoming a new person.

Lamb/5 Pillars

EPILOGUE
BOLL WEEVILS

H.M. Sessions was scared and for good reason. The year was 1915, and his small community of hardworking farmers in southern Alabama was on the verge of bankruptcy. Families he knew and loved had gone from being millionaires to being broke. Too many friends to count had committed suicide due to the bleak outlook, devastating losses, and dashed dreams.

Sessions ran the Farmer & Merchants National Bank in Enterprise, Alabama. Cotton had been king in Coffee County and provided unimaginable wealth to landowners. It was by far the major source of industry and opportunity for the entire region. That is until the boll weevil migrated from Texas and wiped out every crop.

Refusing to give up, Sessions had become obsessed with finding a way out for his family, his business, and the townspeople who had lost any speck of hope. In his search, he came across the writings of Professor George Washington Carver at nearby Tuskegee University. Carver preached the vast and wide-ranging opportunities of the hardy peanut. He believed peanuts were ideal for the Alabama soil and could withstand the Alabama heat and the pesky boll weevil.

Sessions convinced a local farmer who was indebted to his bank to give the peanut a try. The results were immediate. Carver was right. That initial crop produced 9,000 bushels of peanuts, enough for the farmer to pay off his entire debt. The following year, every farm in the region planted peanuts.

Within two years, Coffee County became the largest peanut producer in the entire nation. If you travel the backcountry roads of south Alabama today, peanut farms are nearly as numerous as pine trees. Today 180,000 acres of peanuts are grown in Alabama and contribute over 200 million dollars to the state's economy. The peanut has produced far more wealth and massive amounts of jobs, opportunity, and prosperity in the region than cotton ever did or could.

WHAT'S YOUR BOLL WEEVIL?

You may not know a single thing about farming or peanuts, but have you had intensive experience with boll weevils? If you live long enough, your life will be attacked by a boll weevil. Your pesky insect may take the form of divorce, job loss, abusive relationships, bankruptcy, business failures, or something else.

Those farmers in the South would never have asked for a boll weevil in a million years, but the prosperity and opportunity that followed it was the stuff of dreams. Is it possible your boll weevil is a blessing in disguise? I know you don't even want to consider it, but is there a way to use your most painful life event for something good? I am convinced that the only difference between H.M. Sessions and everyone who neither searched for nor found a solution was Session's mindset. Where others only saw loss, problems, and devastation, Sessions saw a problem to be solved and an answer to be found.

I hope and pray that my book wakes you up and opens your mind to what's possible so that you realize the promise of your future is as real as the pain of your past. You will never convince me otherwise. I have seen too many people come from too far back, overcome the direst of circumstances, and pick themselves up from the fiercest blow to believe otherwise. Your life has a story that is still being written, and you have the pen.

So where do you want to go from here? Do you want to be defined by where you've been or where you're going? Do you want someone else to have the power to determine your defining moment, or are you ready to take that power back? Are you tired of allowing your pain to silence your song, and are you ready to stand up and sing again? The choice is yours, and the power is within you right now. This is the moment. The future you want to create begins today. Go live your life and become fully alive to the opportunities that await.

1. Set your vision.
2. Choose your healthy Lifestyle
3. Find your community in rich relationships.
4. Commit to a fulfilling career that brings you joy.
5. Discover your BIG Mission

These five pillars are the foundation of a better life. They are a set of strategies that will give flight to a future that is right in front of you. I am proud of you for having the courage to own your past but not allowing it to own your life. I can't wait to hear about the impact you have on the lives of others because of it. Thank you for allowing me to be a part of your journey. -David

Note: *The following pages are especially for you, my new friend and colleague in your journey toward a healthier and more meaningful life...Your Big Mission.*

YOUR ACTION PLAN:

1. Set your vision.

Lamb/5 Pillars

YOUR ACTION PLAN

2. Choose your healthy lifestyle

YOUR ACTION PLAN

3. Find your community in rich relationships.

Lamb/5 Pillars

YOUR ACTION PLAN

4. Commit to a fulfilling career that brings you joy.

Lamb/5 Pillars

YOUR ACTION PLAN

5. Discover your BIG Mission.

Lamb/5 Pillars

Lamb/5 Pillars

Lamb/5 Pillars

Lamb/5 Pillars

Lamb/5 Pillars

www.ingramcontent.com/pod-product-compliance
Lightning Source LLC
Chambersburg PA
CBHW050322010526
44119CB00003B/68